MW01680483

DAUGHTERS

Finding God's Heart for His Daughters

Kim Schmelzer

Copyright © 2017 Kim Schmelzer

All rights reserved.

ISBN-13:978-0984660223

DEDICATION

To my father Vincent James Coffaro
Thank you for your faithful love and dedication to our family.
You are my hero.

To my husband Stephen Joseph Schmelzer
Thank you for being a wonderful father to our 4 children and to many other sons and daughters.
You are my love!

CONTENTS

ACKNOWLEDGMENTS

THANK YOU!

To my children:
Jacob and Bethany Schmelzer for believing I could do it!
Natalie Aman for making it look beautiful (and Riley for sharing her)!
Geno and Ali Schmelzer for your inspiration and creative ideas;
Johnny Schmelzer for cheering me on!

To my friends:
Jamee Pineda for being the best editor and cheerleader a friend could ever ask for!
Pete Miller for last-minute proofreading!

To my husband:
Thanks for loving me and being such a great inspiration, and especially for letting me use you and your stories in the book!

To my God:
You are the best Father a girl could ever have! Thanks for encouraging me to do this!

INTRODUCTION:

DADDY'S LITTLE GIRL

April 25, 1981 – The day I had dreamed of had finally come. I had been the little girl who watched movies like Cinderella and Snow White over and over and dreamed of Prince Charming coming to sweep me off my feet. Today, little girls sing "Let it go" and other songs from Disney movies. In my era, I sang "I could have danced all night" from *My Fair Lady*. I wanted to be Julie Andrews when I grew up, and I knew the lyrics to most of the songs from musicals like *The Sound of Music*, *Oklahoma,* and of course, *My Fair Lady*.

Bride magazine and I were best friends! And now it was here, my wedding day, with my own Prince Charming fresh from Oregon. I remember shaking with excitement in the dressing room, peeking out of the door to see who was coming, so excited to walk down that aisle. The smile on my face went clear to my toes. And then it was time. I remember lining up with the wedding party and then I saw him...my dad.

My dad looked so handsome in his tux as he put his arm through mine and we prepared to take that walk down the aisle. I didn't notice it then – the tentative smile, the deep emotion as he looked into my smiling face. I was too focused on this day. It wasn't until later when I saw the pictures that I realized how different that walk was for him. The man who had loved me, protected me, provided for me, and prayed for me was preparing to "give me away" into the arms of another man. I saw that same watery smile in pictures as he "gave away" each of my sisters.

My Sicilian Father

My dad was my hero. He was Sicilian, born to first-generation immigrants from Sicily. I loved to hear stories of his early life. His dad was the pastor of small Italian Pentecostal congregations from the 1930s to the 1950s. His mother was the typical Italian mother, rolling pasta and drying it all over the house. In those days there was a lot of prejudice against various immigrants, including Italians. There was also prejudice against the "Holy Rollers" or early Pentecostals. Dad was not allowed to play sports, go to movies or do much of anything outside of church and school. He chafed against the restrictions and entered the Navy at 17, eventually fighting as an "Amphibian" in WW2.

Dad told stories of his times in China, life on the Navy ship and his prowess as a Navy boxer. He was strong, handsome, and full of life. He came home from the war, married, and had 5 children. He was not serving God, and through a series of events, ended up divorced. He soon met my mother, who was only 16 at the time, and they married. I was born about 15 months later. They were in divorce court before I was 6 months old. Their life was turbulent to say the least. But, my dad did not want to go through a second divorce, so he reached back to his early faith. He committed his life to Jesus and began to pray for his marriage to be restored.

I remember hearing the story of how my dad got the apartment ready for mom's return, putting love notes and welcome home notes in the pots and pans. My mom says she didn't know why at the time, but she went to church with dad and gave her life to God as well. The rest is history. My parents were married for over 50 years, creating a blessed home for my 2 sisters, 4 half brothers, 1 half sister, and me to grow up in. Life was not perfect, but it was good.

I enjoyed a sense of security with my dad and my 4 older

brothers. They were all loving, respectful, and protective of my sisters and me. I never knew a day when they did not love and care for me, so I actually grew up quite naive to the darker side of life that existed for many others. I was a "daddy's girl." I looked forward to dad coming home from work, loved to sit on his lap, listen to his stories and walk on his back! One of my favorite things to do was to cook with my dad (mom too!) and learn the family recipes. We spent countless hours shelling fava beans, forming meatballs, chopping onions and garlic, and making sure the pasta was *al dente.*

Dad had a ready smile and was always singing. He loved to worship and led worship in our home church for many years. He would whistle or play his harmonica while he drove, and I loved to sing along. He was a man of endless energy and an excellent businessman who built several successful enterprises over the years. He loved people and was a generous man with his love, his prayers, and his resources. I was a blessed girl.

My Father God

I take the time to tell you about my dad because I know that my experience is not the norm. So many women have broken relationships with their fathers, as well as other male figures and authorities in their lives. You might have grown up with abuse, neglect, disappointments, or a lack of love and affirmation from a father. The consequences of these run deep and may have kept you from receiving God as the loving Father He is. There have been many studies that detail the consequences related to distant and unloving biological fathers. They range from promiscuity and teen pregnancy to emotional pain, insecurity, and identity issues, to name a few.

Years ago, I had the privilege of hearing a pastor from Ghana, named Dag Heward-Mills. At the time, I picked up a small booklet he had written that changed my life.[1] The booklet spoke of the highest honor and relationship a woman could have with God, which is to be His daughter. As I read the booklet something stirred in my heart. I realized that even with the great example of a dad I had I still felt insecure at times in my relationship with God. I wanted to please Him, to obey and do the things He asked of me. I realized that I had not fully grasped the power and freedom that was mine as a daughter of God.

Through Dag and his writings, I realized that the security and joy I had found from my earthly father was no comparison to the love and blessing I was to enjoy in my relationship with my Father God. I began to ponder this, to remind myself that I was a daughter of God. I had rights and privileges in the family. I was loved and cherished. I was empowered and encouraged. I was asked to join the family business – not as an employee, but as an heir.

You are also a daughter of God! Your natural circumstances don't matter. When you receive Christ as your Lord and Savior, you become part of His family. You are loved, protected, and empowered to join the family business as a daughter and heir.

You will notice as you read that I have included a lot of Bible verses in this book. I do this because they are God's Words and they clearly and powerfully describe Him and His heart for His daughters. I encourage you to read and even memorize these Scriptures. More than anything else, they will help you discover who God is, how He feels about you, and help you find your identity as His daughter. Let's look at what that means, how you can embrace it, and how you can share this good news with other women. But first, what does a girl really want?

CHAPTER 1:

WHAT A GIRL WANTS

My family and I love sappy, feel-good movies, even when they are predictable and have happily- ever- after endings. One such movie is "*What a Girl Wants*," a 2003 comedic drama with Colin Firth and Amanda Bynes. The story goes that Daphne (Amanda Bynes) has never met her father. She feels incomplete and saddened without her dad in her life. She also realizes that she will never experience the traditional father-daughter dance at her wedding. So Daphne travels to London to meet her dad and attempts to fill the deep hole in her heart. She tries everything to please him, including reinventing herself as a proper English debutante, only to find that she can't live as a fake even to win his heart. I don't want to ruin the movie for you, but I will tell you that the father-daughter dance is the stuff fairy tales are made of!

What does every girl want? The list probably includes gift cards, a new wardrobe, and calorie-less chocolate! But on the serious side, what does she really want? Women have needs and desires: physical, spiritual, emotional and relational. We are born with an instinctive sense of need, and God planned for parents to be the first providers for them. Not only the physical needs of food, clothing, and shelter, but more importantly, the spiritual, relational, and emotional needs were to be fulfilled. Love, affection, affirmation, warm hugs, conversation, discipline and direction, Biblical instruction, and values are just some of the gifts that parents were to give their children.

All women want their emotional needs met. In a perfect world, or the world God planned, those needs are first met by her father.

A father's love and affirmation of his little girl form and fortify her sense of identity and security. His protection allows her to grow and stretch her wings. His affirmation secures her and allows her to develop true inner beauty and value. His encouragement provides a foundation for her to explore her gifts and callings and love of learning. His love and words of encouragement allow her to mature and blossom at the right pace. They prevent her from having premature relationships with men because she is not desperate, nor is she looking for love in the wrong time and place. However, many fathers fall short in providing protection and value for their daughters.

Missing Daddy

In an article in *Verily* magazine (online)[1], author Alyssa Elhage shares her own experience of loss after her parents' divorce. She writes about the surprising ways a father impacts who his daughter will marry.

"Like most little girls, my father was my first love. I adored everything about him, even how he smelled (like pine trees and lemons). The sound of his voice on the phone still makes my heart skip a beat. Some of my happiest childhood memories involved listening to his stories about his Lebanese homeland, watching him play silly made-up songs on his guitar, and riding on the front of his bike to the park.

But our time together was bittersweet. After my parents divorced when I was 2, our visits were limited to every other weekend and summer break. I was always overjoyed to see him, but my happiness was marred by sadness because I knew we'd have to say goodbye too soon. Even though I was too young to remember what full-time life with my father was like, those goodbyes hurt so much. Every visit ended with an emotional breakdown for me, so much so that my father would beg, "No crying! You're killing me." I would cling to his shirt anyway, sobbing and breathing in his special smell, overcome with the feeling that my heart—my world—was being torn in two. "

Alyssa shares how much she missed her dad as a child, never knowing how much that would impact her relationships with other men later in life. She says that the world of love and dating was much harder without him guiding her.

She shared the research of Linda Nielsen, Ph.D., professor of education and adolescent psychology at Wake Forest University. Dr. Nielsen has been studying father-daughter relationships for more than a decade, and even teaches a college course on the topic. Ms. Nielsen says that a present, involved father builds up his daughter's self-confidence through encouragement, and his approval stabilizes her desire for other relationships. She says that if a young woman gets that affirmation and approval from her dad, she is not going to be desperate to get it anywhere else because she already has it in him.

Fathers teach us as women that we can be happy on our own without a man—that we are enough by ourselves. Studies show that girls with present and affectionate fathers are *less* likely to develop eating disorders, experience behavioral problems, and become depressed. Of course, not all fathers are affectionate, and some are overly critical, which also robs their daughters of the fatherly affirmation they need. But, overall, growing up in a father-absent home is a major risk factor for depression in teen girls, while having an involved father is linked to fewer psychological problems.

Alyssa shared that her father's absence left a huge void in her heart. She searched for something to fill it, especially through dating. Wanting attention, she often settled for less in a man and found it difficult to trust. She often stayed too long in an unhealthy relationship because she was afraid to let go. When the relationship ended, she fell apart, experiencing episodes of depression. She later shared with a therapist that when her ex broke up with her, she experienced the same kind of panic she had felt as a child when saying goodbye to her dad. I can picture this heartbreaking scene and the pain it leaves in young girls throughout our society.

Dr. Nielsen shared that when young women had weak relationships with their fathers, they often made poor dating choices. She compared father-hunger and dating to going shopping on an empty stomach. “A hungry person makes the worst shopper. You come home with junk food,” she says. “Likewise, a father-hungry young woman will go to the dating supermarket and often come home with the worst men.” Starved for father-love, we too often cling to men who give us the male attention we desire, but, without the example of a strong male character, we fail to be as discerning as we should be.

These last words from Alyssa are so impacting: "My father-hunger issues have given me a deeper appreciation for the irreplaceable role that fathers play in their children’s lives. Today, as I watch my husband interact with our daughter, I am grateful that she is not missing those special moments with him that will shape her life. But what matters the most to me is that she will not spend her life aching for her first love and trying to fill that father-sized hole in her heart with anything else."

Filling the Father-Sized Hole

WOW! I included so many of Alyssa's words because they state the problem so clearly. How many girls are spending their lives "aching for their first love" and trying to fill that "father sized hole" in their heart? It is no wonder that with the increase of divorce and fatherlessness, the cycles of abuse, addiction, and mental illness are increasing. Without a father to love and cherish his little girl, she fails to develop and grow with a healthy sense of worth and value.

Do you find yourself struggling with insecurity? Do you tend to draw back from life and success? Are you overreaching to show that you are enough and don't need anyone to help you succeed? If so, remember that you are a daughter of destiny who is loved by God!

The good news is that you don't have to live with that "father sized hole" forever. While earthly fathers may fail (and even the best will), there is a Father who created and formed you, and each of His daughters. He loves you all more than you can ever imagine. When you receive Him as your father, you will find all that you long for in every area of your life. His love is complete and completing. It fills and fulfills every broken area and place of longing in your life.

Zephaniah 3:17 tells us, *"The LORD your God is in your midst, a mighty one who will save; he will rejoice over you with gladness; he will quiet you by his love; he will exult over you with loud singing.*"

What a beautiful picture of God's love for us. He is our mighty warrior, yet He rejoices over us and quiets us with His love. I get a picture of a father holding his daughter in his arms quieting her with His love. I remember watching my husband, Steve, holding our daughter, Natalie, in his arms. As she grew up, she was always by his side. I have so many pictures of her tucked up next to her dad, quieted and secured by his love for her. Natalie has grown up to be one of the most secure, strong, effective women I have ever met. I am so thankful that she not only has a wonderful relationship with her natural father, but that he wisely led her to a relationship with her heavenly Dad! He is the one who fully gives not only what a girl wants, but what she needs!

In the following chapters I will help you see what a daughter of God looks like. In no way can I give the complete description, but I will paint enough of a picture to help you discover the Father Heart of God toward you and all of His daughters.

DAUGHTERS

Daughters! I absolutely love this word. To be honest, I love words and word games. Bananagrams, boggle, word searches. You name it, I love to play it! Anyone who knows me knows that I also love to use words, a lot of them, and also to form alliterations or acrostics. If I can do a teaching using words that start with the same letter, or take a word and use each letter to share my points, I am in teacher's heaven! My husband and I are pastors of a church we planted in 1981. One thing that was very important to us was providing a place where young men and women could be trained and equipped to find and fulfill what God created them for. To that end, we started an internship and Bible college called ZOE. Each year we have the privilege of spending time with the students and mentoring them. Each year I ask God for a theme to shape my mentoring time with the girls. A few years ago I was impressed to share what it meant to be a daughter of the Lord. I decided to take my love of acrostics and see if I could use it to outline God's heart for His daughters. The following chapters are the result of that! If you enjoy them, maybe we can sit down for a game of bananagrams!

D - DELIGHTED

A - AUTHENTIC

U - UNCONVENTIONAL

G - GLORIOUS WITHIN

H – HONORABLE

T – TRAINED

E – ENERGIZED

R – READY

CHAPTER 2:

DELIGHTED

Delight is an emotion I have enjoyed most of my life. I always had a great imagination and could have a good time with or without other people. I remember a time in first grade. My mother bought me a tent dress. It was the coolest. It was red with huge polka dots, and I could twirl around and watch it swirl around me "with great delight!" The day was cloudy and there were huge puddles on the playground. I twirled and twirled and watched my reflection blend in with the clouds in the huge puddles. I wrote poems in my head. I still remember that feeling of simple, unhindered delight – in my dress, in the crispness of the air, in the joy of twirling. No worries, no cares, no comparisons... pure joy.

The simple dictionary definition of delight is this:

A strong feeling of happiness: great pleasure or satisfaction

Something that makes you very happy: something that gives you great pleasure or satisfaction

Identifying Your Delight

What are some things you delight in? What do you do for people you delight in? How do you think about them?

I delight in my daughter. I really enjoy times together with her - drinking a cup of tea (coffee for her) together, going out to lunch, shopping, trying new restaurants, talking strategy and discipleship, praying for her, worrying about her, and having to trust the Lord where she is concerned. I delight in her. I also have the privilege of having two beautiful daughters-in-law and two incredible granddaughters as well (so far), and they too bring me great delight.

There is a word my husband loves to use to describe this kind of delight - *Naches*.

Naches (נחת) is a Yiddish word that means pride or joy. Typically *Naches* refers to the pride or joy that a child brings a parent. For instance, when a baby is born, people often say to the new parents, "May this child bring you much *Naches*." It literally means to glow with pride.

(FYI - The "ch" is pronounced gutturally, so it's not "ch" as in "cheese" but rather "ch" as in "Bach" (the composer). Most people recognize the style of the "ch" from its use in the words *challah* or *Chanukah*.)

GOD DELIGHTS IN YOU. You bring Him *Naches*. YOU ARE HIS DAUGHTER. He WANTS to bless you, He WANTS to be with you, to hear your voice, to answer your prayers. God wants you to experience delight in the journey of life He created just for you. He knows you, loves you, and ponders you because He delights in you.

Psalm 139 says it so beautifully:

O Lord, you have examined my heart and know everything about me.

You know when I sit down or stand up.

You know my thoughts even when I'm far away.

You see me when I travel and when I rest at home.

You know everything I do.

You know what I am going to say even before I say it, Lord.

You go before me and follow me.

You place your hand of blessing on my head.

Such knowledge is too wonderful for me, too great for me to understand!

I can never escape from your Spirit!

I can never get away from your presence!

If I go up to heaven, you are there; if I go down to the grave, you are there.

If I ride the wings of the morning, if I dwell by the farthest oceans, even there your hand will guide me and your strength will support me.

I could ask the darkness to hide me and the light around me to become night—

but even in darkness I cannot hide from you.

To you the night shines as bright as day.

Darkness and light are the same to you.

You made all the delicate, inner parts of my body and knit me together in my mother's womb.

Thank you for making me so wonderfully complex!

Your workmanship is marvelous—how well I know it.

You watched me as I was being formed in utter seclusion, as I was woven together in the dark of the womb.

You saw me before I was born.

Every day of my life was recorded in your book.

Every moment was laid out before a single day had passed.

How precious are your thoughts about me, O God.

They cannot be numbered!

I can't even count them; they outnumber the grains of sand!

And when I wake up, you are still with me!

O God, if only you would destroy the wicked!

Get out of my life, you murderers!

They blaspheme you; your enemies misuse your name.

O Lord, shouldn't I hate those who hate you?

Shouldn't I despise those who oppose you?

Yes, I hate them with total hatred, for your enemies are my enemies.

Search me, O God, and know my heart; test me and know my anxious thoughts.

Point out anything in me that offends you, and lead me along the path of everlasting life.

Incredible! When I read this Psalm I am overwhelmed. How could the God who created the universe take the time to think about me? How could He have possibly outlined and recorded every day of my life for me, even before I was born? His thoughts for me outnumber the sands of the sea. "Such knowledge is too wonderful for me, too great for me to understand." This is such a perfect description of how God delights in us and how specifically. This knowledge allows us to echo the prayer of David in verses 23-24: "*Search me, O God, and know my heart; test me and know my anxious thoughts. Point out anything in me that offends you, and lead me along the path of everlasting life.*"

I can trust THIS God, MY God to search and know me BECAUSE HE DELIGHTS IN ME. I am His daughter and He finds *Naches* in me.

The following are a few more Scriptures that speak of God's delight in you. I encourage you to read these aloud. Meditate on them. Let the truth and reality of God's delight in You, His beloved daughter, really sink in to the deepest crevices of your heart. Let these truths restore your soul and heal your heart. Let them be like a red tent dress with huge polka dots that makes you want to dance with Your Father and delight in Him.

VERSES:

"Sing, O daughter of Zion; shout aloud, O Israel! Be glad and rejoice with all your heart, O daughter of Jerusalem! For the LORD will remove his hand of judgment and will disperse the armies of your enemy. And the LORD himself, the King of Israel, will live among you! At last your troubles will be over, and you will never again fear disaster. On that day the announcement to Jerusalem will be, "Cheer up, Zion! Don't be afraid! For the LORD your God is living among you. He is a mighty savior. He will take delight in you with gladness. With his love, he will calm all your fears. He will rejoice over you with joyful songs." "I will gather you who mourn for the appointed festivals; you will be disgraced no more. And I will deal severely with all who have oppressed you. I will save the weak and helpless ones; I will bring together those who were chased away. I will give glory and fame to my former exiles, wherever they have been mocked and shamed. On that day I will gather you together and bring you home again. I will give you a good name, a name of distinction, among all the nations of the earth, as I restore your fortunes before their very eyes. I, the LORD, have spoken!" Zephaniah 3:14-20 NLT

"If the Lord delights in us, then He will bring us into this land and give it to us... a land which flows with milk and honey." Numbers

14:8

"The Lord delighted only in your fathers, to love them..." Deut. 10:15

"The Lord your God will delight in you if you obey his voice and keep the commands and decrees..." Deut. 30:10

"He delivered me because he DELIGHTED in me." 2 Samuel 22:20

"As for the saints on the earth - They are the excellent ones in whom is all my delight." Psalm 16:3

"He led me to a place of safety; he rescued me because he delights in me." Psalms 18:19

"Great is the Lord who DELIGHTS in blessing his servant with peace." Ps. 35:27

"The Lord directs the steps of the godly - He delights in every detail of their life..." Psalms 37:23 NLT

Delighting in God

There is a second part to being delighted. Not only does God delight in us, but we are to delight in Him. Psalm 37:4 (NLT) says, "Take delight in the Lord, and he will give you your heart's desires." The Hebrew word for delight means to bend or incline towards or to take pleasure in. We are to incline towards God and take great delight in Him. It is interesting to see the things that God wants us to delight in. Here are a few of them:

- ***His Word***: God wants us to delight in His written Word and the specific words He speaks to us. David speaks often of how he delights in God's Word. Psalm 119 is a very thorough description of this. Psalms 1 describes the person who delights in God's law as blessed, which means fortunate, prosperous, and favored by God.

- ***His will:*** Jesus quoted Psalm 40:8 when He said that He delighted to do God's will. We are to find our pleasure in doing God's will.
- ***His ways***: It is not just enough to be delighted in what God does for us. We are to delight in His ways, His heart and how He works in our lives.

John Piper is one of my favorite Bible teachers. He describes delighting in God as not just delighting in what God does for us but delighting in Him. He says that when you love God's salvation, you don't say mainly, "God's salvation is great!" You say, "God is great!" And when you experience the steadfast love of the Lord, you don't mainly say, "My lips will praise your steadfast love" You mainly say, "My lips will praise YOU!" In other words, the command is to delight in God himself, and all other blessings we enjoy should lead us to God himself as our final and fullest satisfaction...God is most glorified in you when you are most satisfied in Him.

God is our delight. In His presence is fullness of joy. It is good to question myself on what I find delight in. What is it that brings me the most satisfaction? God wants us to enjoy the gifts and blessings He gives us, but in the end, He wants our highest praise, our fullest commitment and obedience. He commands it, but He doesn't want us to give these out of duty or obligation, but out of our delight in Him.

Steve and I recently had the privilege of going on a family vacation to Mexico with our four kids, their spouses, and our 3 grandchildren. We had a wonderful time, but the highlight was the pool time with the grandkids. The pure joy and delight on their faces day after day as we swam and played was priceless. Months after returning home, they still talked with joy about

Mexico and the pool days. This time for us was not drudgery or because we had to. It was delight and we can't wait to go again. I do know that vacation and real life are two different things, and it is easier to be delighted on vacation, but the emotions, the expressions of delight from our grandkids toward us were amazing. And I believe this is what God wants from us - childlike delight in Him. He wants us to long to spend time with Him, to hear His voice, to do what He asks us to do. As daughters of the Lord, God wants us to be full of delight, from Him and for Him. He is so deserving of it.

CHAPTER 3:

AUTHENTIC

I was raised in a Christian home from the time I was 6 months old. I fell in love with Jesus and church when I was about 4. My fondest memories revolve around times at church, not just the services but hanging out with my friends while my parents served, falling asleep on or under the pews, being loved by my pastors, and going out to Stickneys restaurant for homemade chicken noodle soup and strawberry pie after services. It was awesome. Over the years, I continued to grow in my faith, but it was between my sophomore and junior year in high school that I made my grownup decision to give Jesus my whole life.

I remember walking through the trees at youth camp, sensing God's presence with me so strong and confirming in my heart that He wanted me to serve Him fully. I was a rather shy teenager, and as I heard God's call, He told me that to accomplish what He had for me, I could not stay shy. I needed to be bold and confident. I had to step out of my comfort zone.

Of course, God tested me in regard to His instructions. For example, I changed schools during my last 2 years of high school –a rather frightening prospect for this shy, insecure girl. For some reason (I think it was God's sense of humor), my peers elected me to student government as the female chaplain for the school. This was crazy because they did not know me! One of the first orders of business was to attend the student council retreat. I was terrified to say the least! One girl befriended me on the school bus on the rather long drive to our destination. She was very outgoing and kind of boisterous. Since she was reaching out to me, I started acting like her or trying to! I elevated my voice, laughed loudly and who knows what else. At some point in those few days, someone came up to me discreetly and asked me why I was trying to act like this girl. This person encouraged me to just be myself. I felt a little embarrassed, but also very appreciative for the kindness of this relative stranger who encouraged me to be myself.

Being Uniquely YOU

The word authentic means real or genuine; not copied or false. It means being true to one's own personality, spirit, or character, and not an imitation. During the student council retreat, I was trying to be like someone else, and sadly, not doing a good job of it because who I was "elected" to be was me! Why is it so hard for us to be ourselves, to be comfortable in our own skin, to be authentic and not an imitation or copy of someone else?

A few years ago, I was with a group of intern girls at our church. We were talking about how much God loves us and how uniquely He had created us. I asked each of them to think of one quality about themselves that they liked. You would have thought I asked them to bench press 500 pounds by their expressions and initial responses. ALL of them said it was too hard to do. I asked them if it would have been hard to share something they did NOT like about themselves and they all agreed that would be easy, a piece of cake! I didn't let them off the hook, and as each one sheepishly vocalized something they "kind of thought might be, possibly could be, hopefully was" a good quality about themselves, I watched their faces and body language. When others in the room encouraged and agreed with them, and even offered personal proof that it was true, they sat up a little straighter, smiled a bit bigger, and grew a little more secure in who they were!

As daughters of God we were never meant to be a cheap copy or imitation of anyone else. As we read in the last chapter, each of us was uniquely and wonderfully created by God. When we accept and find our security in this truth, we can begin to live authentic lives.

Wearing Our Own Armor

There is a story in the Bible that most of us have heard – David and Goliath. Most of the time we use this story to talk about taking down our enemies and being brave. Outside enemies are definitely a problem, but what about those inner Goliaths that plague each of us: things like insecurity, doubt, depression, fear, anxiety, bitterness, and rejection? I Samuel 17 tells the full story and I encourage you to read it, but there is one part of the story I want to focus on.

David was a young man without a lot of experience in traditional warfare. Yet he was confident in God and completely incensed at the disgraceful taunting and defiance of Goliath toward the armies of the living God (emphasis on living!). He had experience as a shepherd guarding his father's sheep, and he had actually killed a lion and a bear to defend them. Initially, David's brothers thought he was just being cocky and presumptuous when he asked what would be done for the man that killed Goliath.

King Saul heard about David and asked to see him. David said, "Let no man's courage fail because of Goliath. Your servant will go out and fight with this Philistine." Saul tried to tell David that he didn't think he was qualified to go and fight against such a seasoned warrior. David answered him with confidence, letting him know of his past victories as a shepherd. He said, "The Lord who rescued me from the paw of the lion and from the paw of the bear, He will rescue me from the hand of this Philistine."

Saul agreed to send David and dressed him in his own garments and armor. I would have loved to be a fly on the wall to see this. The Bible says that David fastened Saul's sword over his armor and tried to walk BUT HE COULD NOT because he was not used to them and they didn't fit! What a sight that must have been! So David took them off, took HIS shepherd's staff in his hand, then chose for himself five smooth stones out of the stream bed. David put the stones in his shepherd's bag and with his sling in hand, approached the Philistine. Most of us know how the story ends! The Philistine giant derided and disparaged David because he was just a young man, but David was confident in His God and confident in whom God had made him to be. David was being his authentic self, a simple shepherd! And with his simple shepherd's sling and just one of the five smooth stones, David took down the mighty Goliath. He even beheaded him with the giant's own sword. WOW!

These are the words David spoke as he faced the giant. "You come to me with a sword, a spear and a javelin, but I come to you in the name of the Lord of hosts, the God of the armies of Israel, whom you have taunted. THIS DAY the Lord will hand you over to me, and I will strike you down and cut off your head. And I will give the corpses of the army of the Philistines this day to the birds of the sky and the wild beasts of the earth, so that all the earth may know that the Lord does not save with the sword or with the spear; for the battle is the Lord's and He will hand you over to us."

David faced this giant in the security of His relationship with His father, and with his authentic self. He did not wear another man's armor. What a lesson for each of us. We will never be able to conquer the giants in our life – those outside or within us -- in someone else's armor or identity. Each of us must find our identity, our authentic self in our God and in who He created us to be.

There were some pretty awesome women in the Bible (daughters!) who found this to be true. Here are just a few:

- **Deborah** (Judges 4, 5) was a mighty judge in Israel who led her people to victory against Sisera and his armies.

- **Jael** (Judges 4:17-23) was the one who actually killed mighty Sisera in her tent by driving a tent peg through his temple.
- **Esther** (Book of Esther) boldly saved her nation from extinction as the queen during a time of captivity.
- **Mary** the mother of Jesus faced ridicule and rejection as the virgin mother of Jesus.
- **Mary and Martha** were two sisters who served and followed Jesus throughout his life and ministry.

And the list goes on...

Choosing Authenticity

Each of these beautiful daughters of God had to choose to walk in the authentic identity God had given them in the midst of opposition, challenges, and fear from within and without. They chose to wear their own armor and uniquely live out the express purpose of God in their lives.

Two goals are set before us in this journey to be authentic:

> **Be like Jesus**: The first step to being who we are called and created to be is learning to be like Jesus. As we allow Him to lead us through His Word, in prayer, through our leaders, through our experiences, through our obedience, we start to look and act like Him. His nature, His values, His thoughts and actions begin to shape us and we are changed into His image. *"See how very much our Father loves us, for he calls us his children, and that is what we are! But the people who belong to this world don't recognize that we are God's children because they don't know him. Dear friends, we are already God's children, but he has not yet shown us what we will be like when Christ appears. But we do know that we will*

be like him, for we will see him as he really is. And all who have this eager expectation will keep themselves pure, just as he is pure." 1 John 3:1-3 NLT

Be yourself: The second step to being who we are called and created to be is to get comfortable being that person. It means actually liking the person God made, with all your quirks and complexities. I like this description from Diane Motti:

"Being authentic means coming from a real place within. It is when our actions and words are congruent with our beliefs and values. It is being ourselves, not an imitation of what we think we should be or have been told we should be. There is no "should" in authentic... Living authentically is not stagnant: it is constantly shifting and taking on new forms. If we truly believe in living an authentic life, then we must continually be learning about ourselves, challenging old beliefs, sorting through our baggage. It is about learning to face fears and doubts, to be able to reach deeply within ourselves to find out what makes our heart sing, our spirit soar. It is finding where our authentic self feels the most alive, free and unburdened — and then having the courage to live from this place."[1] This was definitely a struggle for me. If we are honest, it is a struggle for most of us. Like my intern girls, saying something good about ourselves is not that easy. We are quick to see what is wrong, what we wish was different, what we wish was like someone else. Yet being authentic is NOT being an imitation. It is being genuine and definitely not a copy. Even becoming like Jesus does not require us to live a fake life. When we receive Christ as our Savior and Lord, HE comes to live inside of us. It is HIS life that is to shine out from us through the unique gifts and calling He gave us.

Ephesians 2:5-10 NLT says "*... even though we were dead because of our sins, he gave us life when he raised Christ from the dead. (It is only by God's grace that you have been saved!) For he raised us from the dead along with Christ and seated us with him in the heavenly realms because we are united with Christ*

Jesus. So God can point to us in all future ages as examples of the incredible wealth of his grace and kindness toward us, as shown in all he has done for us who are united with Christ Jesus. God saved you by his grace when you believed. And you can't take credit for this; it is a gift from God. Salvation is not a reward for the good things we have done, so none of us can boast about it. For we are God's masterpiece. He has created us anew in Christ Jesus, so we can do the good things he planned for us long ago."

Think of it. We were given life by God's grace and are actually united with Christ. We can't take credit for this because it is a gift from God. It is not a reward for the good things we have done. And we are God's masterpiece. In Greek it is the word *poiema* from which we get our English word, poem. We are created in Christ Jesus for good works that God prepared ahead of time for us to do. This changes everything. You and I are not accidents or freaks of nature. We are not afterthoughts, has beens, less thans. We were created, chosen, appointed, and destined for a God - given purpose and plan. There are not accidental humans, regardless of your background, experiences, or current circumstances.

There are so many Scriptures throughout the Bible that attest to this. I will include some references at the end of this chapter for you to read and meditate on. But suffice it to say, you are accepted by God and created EXACTLY how He wanted you to be. He knows you, He formed you and He not only loves you but He LIKES you. It is actually insulting to Him when we don't like ourselves!

I am a parent, and I am crazy about all 4 of my children. I know they are not perfect, but to me they are! I love them and if anyone, including themselves, says something critical or negative about them, I am not a happy camper and they will hear about it! God is our parent AND our creator. He formed us, and He is not pleased when we, or anyone else, insult or demean His kids. YOU are a beautiful, chosen, accepted, desired, called daughter of

God. It is time to accept this with the grace by which it was given. It is time to walk authentically as a masterpiece of God.

This will take some time, some effort and some practice. It will take spending time in God's Word and in prayer to discover His call and purpose. It will take choosing the right kind of relationships that will encourage and challenge you to live authentically in Christ. It will take disciplining your mind and inner speech to agree with the words and thoughts that God has for you. But it is worth the effort because when you finally accept and believe the reality that you are God's beautiful daughter, you will begin to live and enjoy ruling and reigning with Him.

I recommend you read and meditate on the following Scriptures:

- Genesis 1:27
- Psalm 8
- Psalm 139
- Isaiah 29:16
- Jeremiah 1:5
- John 1:12
- Romans 8
- I Corinthians 6:19, 20
- Ephesians 1 and 2
- I Peter 2:9, 10
- I John 1

CHAPTER 4:

UNCONVENTIONAL

Have you ever stopped to think about the way God works – how He does what He does and asks us to do the same? I do, mostly when I first wake up. I am one of those early morning people. That's when I remember what I need to do for the day and start making the "lists." That's when I think, write, plan, read my Bible, AND it is usually during these first thoughts that God speaks to me. It is actually a very precious time. On one of those recent mornings, I heard the word Unconventional. I was thinking about how when we go through difficult times, times of warfare and struggle, God proposes unconventional strategies. I thought about various Bible battles and almost chuckled.

- **Abraham** had 318 trained servants when he was called to go against 5 kings and their armies.

- **Gideon,** already insecure and frightened, was asked to downsize his army from 30,000 to 300 and go against the Midian army who had held his nation captive for many years.

- **Joshua** was asked to take a walled city by walking quietly around it for 7 days, then on the 7th day, to walk around it 7 times and blow trumpets and shout.

- **Jesus** was asked to live a perfect life full of love, then give Himself up to an angry mob of his own people and die for the sins of the world. The list goes on and on, but these stories are unconventional.

Ephesians 6 tells us that we don't battle against flesh and blood (real people) but against principalities and powers and spiritual wickedness in high places. That sounds ominous and epic. God gives a list of spiritual armor and that is great, but He also asks us to face our enemies, to face the battle and to STAND. He doesn't give us permission to run, to hide, or even to fight conventionally. He says STAND.

I don't know about you, but that sounds scary to me. I have a pretty active imagination, so when I think about enemies, they take on huge proportions and frightening visuals. The last thing I want to do is just stand there and face them. I want to run. But God says STAND. Let's read these verses:

"A final word: Be strong in the Lord and in his mighty power. Put on all of God's armor so that you will be able to ***stand*** *firm against all strategies of the devil. For we are not fighting against flesh-and-blood enemies, but against evil rulers and authorities of the unseen world, against mighty powers in this dark world, and against evil spirits in the heavenly places. Therefore, put on every piece of God's armor so you will be able to resist the enemy in the time of evil. Then after the battle you will still be* ***standing firm. Stand*** *your ground, putting on the belt of truth and the body armor of God's righteousness. For shoes, put on the peace that comes from the Good News so that you will be fully prepared. In addition to all of these, hold up the shield of faith to stop the fiery arrows of the devil. Put on salvation as your helmet, and take the sword of the Spirit, which is the word of God. Pray in the Spirit at all times and on every occasion. Stay alert and be persistent in your prayers for all believers everywhere."* Ephesians 6:10-18 NLT

Three times God says to stand: Stand firm, standing firm, stand your ground. Let's look closer at each reference.

"Having done all, to stand." The exhortation is first "to withstand," *i.e.,* to resist all distinct attacks; then, when in this we have "done all" that we are from time to time called to do, "to stand," *i.e.,* to plant our feet firmly on the rock, being "steadfast

and unmovable" (1Corinthians 15:58). The one conveys the idea of bravery and activity; the other of calm, well-balanced steadfastness.[1]

The Greek lexicon shows you that the first "stand" is literally to stand firm or stand your ground. The second "stand" can also be translated as resist. It comes from the Greek word *antistenai* from which we get the word for antihistamine, drugs that stand against or resist allergic reactions in the body. The third mention is like the first "*stenai* "which means to stand firm or make a stand. This may seem a little complicated, but it is important. As daughters of our amazing God, He asks us to be like Him, to live, and yes, to war like He does. He even promises to train us for war (Psalms 144). Now that is unconventional! This word means not based or conforming to what is generally done or believed. It means unusual, unorthodox, unfamiliar, and uncommon.

Pillars for the Palace

When my husband dedicates babies, he often uses Psalm 144:12. "May our sons be like plants grown up in their youth and may our daughters be like pillars, sculptured in palace style." He says this describes how God created his daughters to be – strong and useful like a pillar, but beautiful in design, fit for a palace.

I bought a magnet with this phrase: "Well-behaved women rarely make history!" I researched the history of this quote and found out it was from the diary of an ordinary midwife and healer from the late 1700s. Here is the context of this phrase:

"*Cotton Mather called them 'The Hidden Ones.' They never preached or sat in a deacon's bench. Nor did they vote or attend Harvard. Neither, because they were virtuous women, did they question God or the magistrates. They prayed secretly, read the Bible through at least once a year, and went to hear the minister preach even when it snowed. Hoping for an eternal crown, they never asked to be remembered on earth. And they haven't been.*

Well-behaved women seldom make history..." [2]

God's girls are not conventional. They are designed for strength, built to stand, and beautiful, and they do make history.

Being a woman in today's world holds many challenges, as well as opportunities. The world our mothers and grandmothers lived in was much different, especially for females. It is no longer the norm for women to be homemakers. Many have entered the workforce and are moving into higher positions of influence in business and government sectors. While this is not a book about the changing roles of women, it is important to reference the shifts because they have a direct effect on how we operate in modern times. This is seen very clearly in the church today as women begin to move into staff and ministry roles that were previously held only by men. So, how does a woman maintain the Biblical roles of wife and mother and at the same time, step out into the call and plan of God that may be somewhat unconventional?

The Bible is full of great examples of such women. Eve operated side by side with Adam in caring for the Garden of Eden. Deborah was a judge in Israel who helped lead her people into freedom from oppression. There were women in the Bible who prophesied, were businesswomen, teachers, prophetesses and more. There were wives and mothers who carried out their duties with vision and strength. Like the midwives spoken of by Cotton Mather, the Egyptian midwives during Moses' times were instrumental in saving the young Jewish male babies from certain death. It takes women of all ages, with unique gifts and destinies, to help fulfill God's purpose in the earth. We were created by God to be suitable helpers who are capable of sharing the burden, workload and joy of doing God's will alongside capable men created with specific purpose and call.

The Bible gives clear descriptions of what a godly woman should be. I Peter 3:3-5 says it this way: *"Don't be concerned about the outward beauty of fancy hairstyles, expensive jewelry, or beautiful clothes. You should clothe yourselves instead with the beauty that comes from within, the unfading beauty of a gentle and quiet spirit, which is so precious to God. This is how the holy women of old made themselves beautiful. They put their trust in God and accepted the authority of their husbands.*"[2]

This counsel works in all times and all societies. God's daughters don't focus on just looking beautiful on the outside. They remember that they are pillars and develop the unfading beauty of a gentle, quiet spirit, which provides real strength for the roles they are called to fill. God's daughters understand that the submitted life is the best life and that submission opens doors to power and true freedom. They are submitted to God, to their fathers and husbands when they marry, and they are submitted to the call and plan of God on their life. When you agree to submit in this way, the various roles of your life work together and allow you to be a strong and beautiful pillar, able to stand in and through all situations. It may be an unconventional way to live according to the modern, independent woman, but because you are a submitted daughter of God, He provides you with new and exciting opportunities. He dares you to live an unconventional life, and at the same time, promises to protect and defend you. Will you accept the challenge? The world needs more unconventional women who will trust Father God and who are ready to stand and fight for their right to be different.

CHAPTER 5:

GLORIOUS WITHIN

When I read the Bible as a young girl, I usually read and memorized Scripture from the King James Version. The words would roll through my mind and heart. A few verses from Psalm 45 were some of my favorite. The picture of the king's daughter all glorious within captured my heart and imagination. I encourage you to read the whole Psalm but here are the specific verses I focused on from the King James Version:

"Kings' daughters were among thy honourable women: upon thy right hand did stand the queen in gold of Ophir. Hearken, O daughter, and consider, and incline thine ear; forget also thine own people, and thy father's house; So shall the king greatly desire thy beauty: for he is thy Lord; and worship thou him. And the daughter of Tyre shall be there with a gift; even the rich among the people shall entreat thy favour. The king's daughter is all ***glorious within****: her clothing is of wrought gold. She shall be brought unto the king in raiment of needlework: the virgins her companions that follow her shall be brought unto thee. With gladness and rejoicing shall they be brought: they shall enter into the king's palace. Instead of thy fathers shall be thy children, whom thou mayest make princes in all the earth. I will make thy name to be remembered in all generations: therefore shall the people praise thee forever and ever."* Psalm 45:9-17 KJV

While these verses probably refer to the king's daughter being glorious within the palace, I see these words as describing the principle of “inside out" transformation and inner beauty. As I referenced earlier, I Peter 3:3-6 says this:

“Don’t be concerned about the outward beauty of fancy hairstyles, expensive jewelry, or beautiful clothes. You should clothe yourselves instead with the beauty that comes from within, the unfading beauty of a gentle and quiet spirit, which is so precious to God. This is how the holy women of old made themselves beautiful. They put their trust in God and accepted the authority of their husbands. For instance, Sarah obeyed her husband, Abraham, and called him her master. You are her daughters when you do what is right without fear of what your husbands might do.” 1 Peter 3:3-6 NLT

- ***The King's daughter*** –The one who knows who she is and values her place as God's daughter –is glorious within. She has taken the time to develop that hidden person of the heart, the part that is not corruptible, and she has put on the ornament of a meek and gentle and quiet spirit, which is so precious to God.

- ***The King's daughter*** –The one who knows who she is and values her place as God's daughter – is glorious within the placement and protection that God provides for her. That may be her natural family, her church family, or both.

I remember reading these passages over and over, and still to this day, those words ring in my heart. “King's daughters are among your honorable women... Hearken and consider this and incline your ear, forget your own people and your father's house; for HE IS THE LORD, worship Him.” The King's daughter is glorious within, clothing herself with a gentle and quiet spirit. I wanted to be a King's daughter who was honorable, who made God her Lord, her Savior, and worshipped Him with all her heart! I wanted to have a listening ear, an obedient heart that put God and His will for my life first, over family and friends and any other thing. I wanted to be "glorious within."

For some years I tried to do this in my own strength, or at least with a good amount of "I can do it myself," with various levels of trust in the grace of God and the power of the Holy Spirit working in me. I struggled with my identity, with my self-image and worth, with an overactive desire to please and work my way to a glorious King's daughter status. I loved God; I loved to read my Bible and worship. I loved my church family and I longed to be one who God wanted to be with, and to work through.

When I got married, my husband noticed my overactive desire to please. He noticed that when I did something that I deemed wrong, I would beat myself up over it. I remember one day he said to me, "I don't think you understand God's love for you and what He did for you when He saved you." I remember how those words struck me. They were too true to make me angry. He shared his thoughts on God's love for me and what salvation really was, and later I spent time with God searching out what this meant.

The change in me did not happen overnight, but gradually I began to replace my improper understanding of "working out my own salvation" and began to trust in the incredible love and favor that my God, my Father, had for me. As a result, a "King's daughter" was born! I began to apply the Scriptures that speak of God's love and favor, His grace and power in my life, and my thinking process shifted. Insecurity gave way to inner security; independence gave way to "In - dependence" on my Father. This prayer of the Apostle Paul became so real, so precious to me:

"When I think of all this, I fall to my knees and pray to the Father, ***(MY FATHER)*** *the Creator of everything in heaven and on earth. I pray that from his glorious, unlimited resources he will empower you with inner strength through his Spirit. Then Christ will make his home in your hearts as you trust in him. Your roots will grow down into God's love and keep you strong. And may you have the power to understand, as all God's people should, how wide, how long, how high, and how deep his love is. May you experience the love of Christ, though it is too great to understand fully. Then you will be made complete with all the fullness of life and power that*

comes from God. Now all glory to God, who is able, through his mighty power at work within us, to accomplish infinitely more than we might ask or think. Glory to him in the church and in Christ Jesus through all generations forever and ever! Amen." Ephesians 3:14-21 NLT

I love to highlight and underline bold words that are special to me. If I had this freedom with Scripture, THIS WHOLE PASSAGE WOULD BE MARKED UP! The words are so life changing if we let them sink in. I AM A KING'S DAUGHTER! God IS MY FATHER! I want to let my roots grow down deep into God's love and it will keep me strong. I want to have the power to know how wide, how long, how high, and how deep His love is and to EXPERIENCE His love in all its grandeur. And the best news of all is that HE is able through HIS mighty power, which is ALREADY WORKING in me to accomplish INFINITELY MORE than I can even ask or think. Now that is good news!

What is the result of this? I am "glorious within," not because of the good works I have done. I am "glorious within" because I have received the finished work of Jesus Christ to save me and ransom me from the kingdom of darkness into the kingdom of Light, His kingdom. I am no longer a slave, no longer a fearful little girl trying to "get it together." I am a King's daughter and HE has made me glorious within His house and within my heart.

When my kids were little I would ponder them. I would tell them I loved them and sometimes when I hugged them, I would pray they would understand "how wide, how deep, how high," my love was for them. I couldn't squeeze them hard enough or use enough loving words to fully describe my heart towards them. It was too great. Even though they are grown, I still feel the same, and now that love has spilled over into the grandkids. And that love is just a thimbleful compared to the love our Father has for us.

My prayer for you, daughter of the Lord, is that you would take the time to let this truth sink deep into the crevices and cavities of your soul. Let it sink in and drown the insecurities, the fears, the "overactive- trying to please" parts of you and fill you with gladness and amazement. The beautiful result of this is found in the end of Psalms 45. "*Instead of thy fathers shall be thy children, whom thou mayest make princes in all the earth. I will make thy name to be remembered in all generations: therefore shall the people praise thee for ever and ever.*"

YOUR children, natural and spiritual, will be princes and princesses in the earth for generations to come. The Kingdom of God will be extended by "King's daughters and sons" who know their Father and are immersed in His love and favor.

Please read the following passage to yourself and then read it out loud, replacing the "You" with your name. Read it more than once and let the incredible truths of what Christ has done for you and in you build a strong foundation in your mind and heart. This is how we become King's daughters who are glorious within!

"You used to live in sin, just like the rest of the world, obeying the devil—the commander of the powers in the unseen world. He is the spirit at work in the hearts of those who refuse to obey God. All of us used to live that way, following the passionate desires and inclinations of our sinful nature. By our very nature we were subject to God's anger, just like everyone else. But God is so rich in mercy, and he loved us so much, that even though we were dead because of our sins, he gave us life when he raised Christ from the dead. (It is only by God's grace that you have been saved!) For he raised us from the dead along with Christ and seated us with him in the heavenly realms because we are united with Christ Jesus. So God can point to us in all future ages as examples of the incredible wealth of his grace and kindness toward us, as shown in all he has done for us who are united with Christ Jesus. God saved you by his grace when you believed. And you can't take credit for this; it is a gift from God. Salvation is not a reward for the good things we have done, so none of us can boast about it. For we are God's masterpiece. He has created us anew in Christ Jesus, so we can do the good things he planned for us

long ago." Ephesians 2:2-10 NLT

There was a popular Christian singer in the late 1970s and early 80s named Evie Tornquist. She was a tiny 4'11" powerhouse whose songs captured my generation. She sang a song called "He loves me," which impacted me greatly. I would sing it over and over and rejoice in the incredible reality of God's love for me.

"Well, he loves me! And that´s a brand new story.

He loves me! And that´s a brand new song.

He loves me! He loves me! He loves me!

And I just can´t keep from singing.

And you ask me do I need him?

Well, does a river need the water to get along?

Mine was a life that didn´t begin until Jesus.

It only began the moment that he became real.

Now there´s a joy that has taken me over completely.

No one can know just how special that he makes me feel."[1]

Within the Palace

The second reality is that the King's daughter is glorious within the palace. I believe that our placement in the body of Christ is essential for our health and development. Psalm 45 says that this daughter lives in His palace, His house. It is so important that you find a local church where you can be planted securely. We all need healthy relationships and leaders to help us grow. The local church is where you will be connected to God through His people and where who you are on the inside finds its outward expression.

I read an interesting blog by Kevin Harney. He shared the following conversation he had with a young woman concerning her involvement in church. He asked her where she went to church. She replied that she had three main churches. She loved the music at one, attended a small group at another and loved the "nice people" and enjoyed the singles ministry at another. He asked her again where she went to church. I loved his next question: “Where do you invest yourself, serve, give and do community as part of God's family?” This opened up a healthy dialogue which concluded with the young woman admitting that she had really looked at church as a place to get her needs met. She admitted that she had never been engaged as a servant. How many of us can identify with this young woman? Her lack of commitment and engagement would never produce the legacy and fruitfulness described in Psalm 45.

You have the privilege of allowing God to work His will in you and through you. You can choose to invest yourself within His church. Yes, it will require sacrifice and commitment, but the reward is worth it. You will never be truly whole and complete without finding your place in God's body. I Corinthians 12 talks about how every part of the body is significant and needed. It is your interaction with your church family – as you serve and learn, as you give and receive, that real growth and life change happens. You can't successfully be a Christian all by yourself. God didn't design you to be alone. In fact, He said it wasn't good! We are more glorious and better together.

What are some of the glorious things you can expect when you allow both parts of this spiritual equation to work in you? Your life is marked by glorious praise (Psalm 66), glorious, inexpressible joy (I Peter 1:8), and Christ in you the hope of glory (Col. 1:27). You are able to be a part of a glorious church that is bringing heaven to earth through all generations (Eph. 3:21). You are glorious within and without!

CHAPTER 6:

HONORABLE

If you have been in or around church a while, you have most likely heard of the Proverbs 31 woman. If you have not, let me fill you in! The last chapter of the book of Proverbs describes what many Christians call "Wonder woman." This gal is an awesome wife and mother who takes incredible care of her family. She is an entrepreneur who is gifted in business, yet gets up before dawn to make sure her family is clothed and fed. She is diligent, compassionate, and generous with those in need.

The Proverbs 31 woman speaks with wisdom and kindness, and she is emotionally well adjusted, looking with joy towards the future. If you haven't read about her, I encourage you to spend some time getting acquainted with her. The end result for this woman is that her husband and children stand and bless her, plus her honorable life earns praise and respect by all who know her.

I have heard many women talk about the immense pressure this woman has put on them! They often ask, “How can I possibly live up to someone like her?” Well, I answer that question this way: The Proverbs 31 woman is the ideal, based on the full life journey of a Godly woman. Since we have not lived our full life yet, we are in a process. And while this offers some relief, the life of a Proverbs 31 woman is still a tall order!

What I learn from Mrs. 31 is that she has chosen to live an honorable life. She is a daughter of great honor. The definition of honor is something of value, something to respect and esteem. So we see that this woman's life is full of value.

As I prepared to write this chapter, I had a few different words for the letter H. I considered humble and honest, but then I realized that the word honor encompasses them both. A woman of honor is honest and she is humble. Where does this honorable life come from? It comes from a life lived with value: giving value to God, to your own life, to others, and to the value system that fuels you. An entire book could be written about honor, but let's look at four areas the Proverbs 31 woman expresses honor. Let's at least start the dialogue.

She Honors God

This honorable woman honors and fears the Lord, which fuels everything she does. She puts God first and values His will and approval more than any other. It is so easy to honor other people's opinion more than God's. "*Fearing man is a dangerous trap, but trusting the Lord means safety.*" Proverbs 29:25

As women, we are often given to comparison. We are overly concerned with pleasing others and desperately crave their approval. So we find ourselves in never-ending cycles that make us feel like we have failed and sometimes keep us from the success and approval we desire. The woman who honors the Lord has made a decision to live by a different value system. She has chosen to find her worth first from God, and then from honoring the life plan He shows her. Proverbs 31:10 says that her worth is far above rubies. By honoring God she finds honor – lasting honor and approval from all the right sources.

She Honors Herself

"*She is clothed with strength and dignity, and she laughs without fear of the future. When she speaks, her words are wise, and she gives instructions with kindness.*" Proverbs 31:25-26 NLT

These verses from Proverbs 31 are some of my favorite. They have become a pattern for me to align my life because they represent the lifestyle and mindset of a woman of honor. The word dignity actually means a quality of living worthy of honor or respect. Strong and dignified, Mrs. 31 smiles at the future. Her words both give value and are valuable because they are wise and kind. She doesn't look for outside approval because she is comfortable in her own skin. She enjoys being the woman God created her to be.

She Honors Others

A woman of honor puts others first, even if it means getting up before dawn to take care of their needs! It isn't just in her actions but also through her words. I love the quote from the movie *The Help.* It says, "You is kind. You is smart. You is important." When we speak words of encouragement, they become words of life to others because we are imparting value to them. Romans 12:9,10 says it this way, *"Don't just pretend to love others. Really love them. Hate what is wrong. Hold tightly to what is good. Love each other with genuine affection, and take delight in honoring each other."*

I also like this version of Romans 12:9-10. *"This is how I want to live – not with pretense but in reality by giving value to those around me. This includes my friends and family, the leaders in my life and even those who are strangers to me. When I see and place value in others my life will have value as well."*

Another way we honor others is by valuing the strengths and gifts of everyone. My husband taught this principle to our children in regards to receiving words from other people. He referenced Matthew 10:41: *"If you receive a prophet as one who speaks for God, you will be given the same reward as a prophet. And if you receive righteous people because of their righteousness, you will be given a reward like theirs."*

Steve taught that we need to honor the gift in others. Some people will honor God but live independently and without appreciation of the gifts in others. They don't honor the words and counsel from their leaders, nor do they receive and appreciate the special gifts that others have, or they take them for granted. One example of how we taught our children to apply the principle of appreciation and honor was in relation to their music teachers. We challenged them to dig deep and learn all they could, to show respect and appreciation for their teacher's excellence. We paid the teachers cheerfully, even when we had to miss a lesson. We didn't complain about wasting money, but instead shared with our children that payment was the least we could do for the honor of receiving from them. Why? Because when you believe in and honor your music teacher, you will get their best and actually receive an impartation of their excellence. This principle of honor and appreciation pays dividends in every area of life. Give value and you will receive value –usually multiplied many times over.

She Honors Values

A woman of honor aligns her life with a system of values that bring her honor in return. This system is a set of principles that guide her behavior and choices. Everyone will have certain values that are unique to them, but there are some that are non-negotiable and transcend social, economic, and religious boundaries. These are values like integrity, honesty, and humility. Self-control and responsible living are also non-negotiable.

It is crucial to identify the values that will guide your decisions and behaviors, and then hold onto them for all you are worth. God's Word is a great source for the principles and values that will give structure and purpose to your life.

There will be other unique values you will live by, many that will mark your life and the lives of those you influence. My parents and my husband's parents placed huge value on hospitality. They were always having people over to share a meal, so our tables were marked with excellence and lots of food! We have a saying in our family, "If you bless, really bless," which means give your best and don't just do the bare minimum. That is a family value.

Another value of our family is open communication. We refuse to live with a lot of unresolved issues, so we practice talking things through and seeing healthy conflict as a good thing. This wasn't easy for me at first. I didn't like to make waves, but I began to see the value of talking things through and not leaving a lot of "elephants in the room." It is important to identify the unique family values that are part of your life and share them with others. We honor one another when we appreciate the differences and learn and grow from each other.

These 4 areas are a good place to start in building a life that honors God. Like the Proverbs 31 woman, it will be a journey that will take a lifetime. To be a woman who fears the Lord and honors Him in every area of life is to find the value He intended for you. To live a valueless, self-absorbed life is to lose the very essence of why we were created.

Mary, an Honorable Woman

A woman in the Bible who demonstrated a life of honor was Mary, the mother of Jesus. When I line her life up against the above 4 areas of honor, I see a woman whose life I can follow. She honored God fully. In Luke 1:38, the angel told Mary she was going to be the mother of the Messiah. She answered, "Be it unto me according to Your word."

She HONORED God through her obedience to be the mother of Jesus as God asked, and she honored God throughout her life, never wavering in her belief in Jesus.

Mary HONORED herself by doing what God asked of her and not fearing what man would say. She knew that being pregnant without being married would open her up to much shame and condemnation from others, yet she chose to believe God and believe His words that she was highly favored.

Mary HONORED others by encouraging them to follow Jesus. At the wedding of Cana, she told the servants to do whatever Jesus asked them to do, and a miracle followed.

She HONORED her values. She chose to obey God no matter what, with no worry about personal cost. I want to be like Mary and honor God in all I do.

I Samuel 2:30 says that he who honors God will be honored. I have had the privilege of knowing many women who chose honor. Their lives were not perfect or without struggle and pain, but they had value. The heart of their husbands safely trusted in them and their children openly blessed them. They may not have had all the money or fame that so many place value in but their worth was far above rubies. I want to be that woman and bring glory to my Father.

Each of you can choose to live clothed with dignity and honor. It is a path built step by step through daily decisions to put God first. It means choosing to honor the unique person God has created you to be and not falling into the trap of comparison or envy. You will find your joy as you encourage others through acts of service and words of encouragement. There will be struggles and mistakes but the journey will be marked clearly with the values you live by; you will be able to get back on course. You will embrace the past, present and future of your life with a smile because that is the blessing of an honorable life and it is a life worth living.

CHAPTER 7:

TRAINED

We have a phrase in our family that has become legendary – "Uncle Steve say NO." Here's how the legend started: My husband Steve and I were babysitting our nephew Nathan. He was quite young, and in the course of the day, my husband told him no. This made quite an impression on his young mind. He later told his mom in his little voice with much emotion, "Uncle Steve say NO." She shared this with us later and we have laughed and repeated the story for many years.

We may have laughed, but there is a lot to be said for the word "No." In fact, to be a child of God, you must be able to hear and respond to God's "NO" if you are going to walk in the "Yes" He has planned for your life.

Don't just take my word for it. Here are a few of many Scriptures that describe this process. I take the time to print them out because they speak so directly and clear.

"*My children, listen when your father corrects you. Pay attention and learn good judgment, for I am giving you good guidance. Don't turn away from my instructions. For I, too, was once my father's son, tenderly loved as my mother's only child. My father taught me, "Take my words to heart. Follow my commands, and you will live. Get wisdom; develop good judgment. Don't forget my words or turn away from them.*" Proverbs 4:1-5 NLT

"*In this all-out match against sin, others have suffered far worse than you, to say nothing of what Jesus went through—all that bloodshed! So don't feel sorry for yourselves. Or have you forgotten how good parents treat children, and that God regards you as his children? My dear child, don't shrug off God's discipline, but don't be crushed by it either. It's the child he loves that he disciplines; the child he embraces, he also corrects. God is educating you; that's why you must never drop out. He's treating you as dear children. This trouble you're in isn't punishment; it's training, the normal experience of children. Only irresponsible parents leave children to fend for themselves. Would you prefer an irresponsible God? We respect our own parents for training and not spoiling us, so why not embrace God's training so we can truly live? While we were children, our parents did what seemed best to them. But God is doing what is best for us, training us to live God's holy best. At the time, discipline isn't much fun. It always feels like it's going against the grain. Later, of course, it pays off handsomely, for it's the well-trained who find themselves mature in their relationship with God.*" Hebrews 12:4-11 MSG

Correction and Consequences

God commands natural parents to correct and train their children while they are young. One class I teach regularly is "Parenting," which speaks about the necessity and commitment to godly correction as foundational training. Clear boundaries with clear consequences consistently communicated while the child is young produce well-adjusted, secure children who know they are loved. Interestingly enough, this translates into their relationship with God. If they can respond to their parents' "No's," it is much easier for them to respond to God's training and correction. They understand that correction is not rejection, but a true sign of acceptance and paternity.

Recently, my husband and I were talking with our son Geno. He was sharing something he noticed about certain struggles of those who did not have a strong father in their lives. He said, "There is something that is formed in you when your father brings correction." Geno described how a father imparts something priceless into his children when they realize they are not the boss, that they are not all-powerful. All four of our children have related this same concept in different ways. There is something essential that godly correction brings to our lives. Without it, we cannot mature and will never fully understand or receive God's love for us.

In a "Focus on the Family" article, author Glenn Stanton highlights the importance of an involved father.[1] The article outlines some of the differences mothers and fathers bring to parenting. *"Educational psychologist Carol Gilligan tells us that fathers stress justice, fairness and duty (based on rules), while mothers stress sympathy, care and help (based on relationships). Fathers tend to observe and enforce rules systematically and sternly, teaching children the consequences of right and wrong. Mothers tend toward grace and sympathy, providing a sense of hopefulness....Involved dads help children see that attitudes and behaviors have consequences. For instance, fathers are more likely than mothers to tell their children that if they are not nice to others, kids will not want to play with them. Or, if they don't do well in school, they will not get into a good college or secure a desirable job. Fathers help children prepare for the reality and harshness of the world."*[1]

As daughters of God we must ask ourselves some questions:

- Am I Teachable?
- Do I love to learn?
- How do I respond to correction?
- How do I respond to praise?

Your answers to these questions tell a lot about your relationship with Father God. It is the child He loves that He corrects. It is the child that knows and accepts this that responds correctly and is well-trained. Proverbs 12:1 says it clearly: *"To learn, you must love discipline; it is stupid to hate correction."*

The Joy of Tests

I loved taking tests in school. They were like a game to me, and even the initial anxiety I felt before testing was part of the fun. I remember homeschooling my children, and at the end of each year, I would have them tested to see how they were progressing. Each one responded differently to tests. My daughter didn't enjoy them very much and at first it surprised me. Then I started thinking about testing so that I could help reduce her stress. I remember the "aha moment" when I realized the purpose of testing. It wasn't just a game to be won. It wasn't to show how much you don't know in order to make people feel stupid. No, it was to show people where they could continue to learn. It was a tool to help people grow, to show them where they lacked knowledge so they could develop a strategy or curriculum to help them learn. It was a gift, a reward to help people, and not a punishment to hurt them. The sooner we realize this about the tests and training God gives us, the more we can learn and grow.

"*Consider it a sheer gift, friends, when tests and challenges come at you from all sides. You know that under pressure, your faith-life is forced into the open and shows its true colors. So don't try to get out of anything prematurely. Let it do its work so you become mature and well-developed, not deficient in any way.*" James 1:3, 4 MSG

Teachable

One example of a well-trained, teachable son was Timothy. Paul called him his son in the faith and he trusted him to train others. How do we know Timothy was teachable? It is because he was able to be taught and teach others. That is the sign of a well-trained person. 2 Timothy 2 gives us some qualities to look for.

Trained people are:

1. Strong in grace

2. Able to suffer as a soldier (Endurance)

3. Able to compete like an athlete (Winning attitude)

4. Able to work like a farmer (Hardworking/Fruitful)

5. Faithful, loyal and honest

6. Not given to useless arguments and disputes

7. Pure in lifestyle (Not Entangled)

8. Have Godly relationships (Iron Sharpens Iron)

9. Servants who love God and love people – speaks truth in love

10. Able to teach...even difficult people

Take some time to read 2 Timothy 2. Examine your own life to see if these qualities are growing in your life. Ask yourself how you receive correction. Do you have "test anxiety," or do you understand the purpose and blessing behind every challenge? Reread the Scriptures in this chapter and make sure you understand God's heart toward you. When God says "No," do you understand it is just part of the path to His "best yes" for your life?

Another aspect of training is being teachable. I believe that a love of learning is a non-negotiable quality for God's daughters. Curiosity, a thirst for knowledge, a desire to grow should be strong in us. Jesus said that if we wanted to be part of His kingdom, we needed to become like little children. I know there are many interpretations of this, but I believe one is this sense of wonder and discovery. I had the privilege of hearing Liz Wiseman talk about this from her book *Rookie Smarts.* This book encourages and trains you to get back to the curious, flexible, youthful mindset that you had when you started your Christian walk. The Bible calls this your "first love."

One criticism of the church in Ephesus from the book of Revelations is that they lost their "first love.' Is it possible to get crusty and inflexible in our walk with God? Can we lose our sense of wonder and the hunger and thirst for God that keeps us moving forward? Yes, we can. And we often do. Staying teachable keeps us open to new discoveries. It keeps us hungry and thirsty for more. Author Liz Wiseman recommended that we literally get on the ground to look at things from the view of a small child. I tried it, and it was amazing how different everything looked, from the smallest bug, to the patterns in foliage, and the possible adventures in a puddle.

My husband is a great example to me in this area. I can get stuck in a rut and want to keep things nice and tidy and safe. He is always studying about something and trying new things. He studied fermentation and learned to make sauerkraut, kefir and apple cider vinegar. He learned how to make our own soap and he conducted research to find a special Castile soap that would be fit for his "princess." He takes apart computers, and puts them back together. He learned to sail, and flies stunt kites. He even plays the harmonica.

Steve doesn't become an expert at everything he does, but the process of learning and growth is a home run! Everyone who knows him laughingly asks what he is studying now and enjoys his journeys into the unknown. It has been amazing over the years how God has used his hobby studies to open conversations with all kinds of people that eventually allow him to share his faith. His "Rookie Smarts" encourage me to think deeper, study things out, and to not take things at face value. This not only helps in learning, but also has carried over into relationships. It has helped me be more open to learn from others, and in doing so, I have found unexpected treasures of knowledge and enjoyed new friendships.

Training is a lifelong process. Albert Einstein said this: *"Intellectual growth should commence at birth and cease only at death."* Solomon said that *the path of the just is like a shining light that shines more and more till the fullness of day.* I believe that if we keep learning, and keep being trained, that our path gets clearer and the journey more fulfilling. One writer said that being teachable is the most important life skill. When we stay teachable, we stay flexible. We are not arrogant and proud, but aware and humble Teachable people know their own limitations but are willing to step out and take risks. They don't give up and are continually learning from whoever and whatever they can. Boredom is rare.

Here are a few practical tips for you. Stay positive and try to learn something new regularly. Surround yourself with people that stretch you. You can do this in person but also through blogs, podcasts, books, and conversations via social media. The book of James tells us not to just be hearers of God's Word but doers. This principle applies to all areas of healthy training. John Maxwell has a book entitled *Sometimes you win; Sometimes you learn*. Being teachable is a choice. Let's make sure we choose correctly!

CHAPTER 8:

ENERGIZED

In 1989 an advertising *phenom* was born, called the Energizer Bunny. We have all seen the little pink bunny beating its drum and going and going and going. The marketing thought was that just like this energized, nonstop bundle of energy kept going, so would every other item powered by Energizer batteries! Toys, cameras, flashlights – you name it, they were energized. People enjoyed watching commercials featuring the Energizer Bunny and bought into the marketing campaign. It was such a success that *Advertising Age* magazine added the Energizer Bunny to its list of the top 10 brand icons of the 20th century, citing him as "*the ultimate symbol of longevity, perseverance and determination.*"[1]

Most women I know wish they had the energy of this pink *phenom*! With all the responsibilities and multitasking going on, a lifetime supply of Energizer batteries would come in handy. Gals have a never-ending list of "to dos," from morning to night and that is only physical responsibilities. It takes energy and work to stay sharp intellectually and spiritually, not to mention keeping relationships healthy and emotions stable. I am getting tired just thinking about it!

What Would a Princess Do?

But we are God's daughters. Doesn't that make us princesses? Do princesses even have to work? I found a fun blog titled "*What would Kate do?*" authored by Amanda (she didn't give her last name). It is an upbeat site with lots of great information about Princess Kate. In one blog she talked about some of the requirements for today's princess. They need a university degree from a good school, need to speak at least a second language, have excellent social skills, give significant support to charities, be well-versed in a wide variety of art, music and culture, be an excellent communicator, and the list goes on.

Maybe your life is not the stuff fairy tales are made of, but you still have a lot to accomplish. In fact, most women put unrealistic expectations on themselves based on what the "perfect woman" should do and be. In today's world, many women are juggling marriage, family, and careers while trying to be gourmet chefs, fashion divas, and still find time for romance and friendly coffee dates!

I was one of those "I can do it all and do it myself" kind of women. It worked pretty well for me growing up. I got good grades in school, had good friends, and was able to keep all the balls in the air. I got married and juggled work, home, and church like a champ. Steve and I pioneered a church one year after we were married, and 2 years later our first son, Jacob, was born. The pressure was on to be the perfect wife, mother, pastor's wife, chef, housekeeper, friend, and other things too numerous to list. Mind you, this pressure was not coming from anyone else. It was all coming from inside of me. It was getting harder, but I was that Energizer Bunny and I just kept going and going and going.

I suffered a miscarriage about a year and a half after Jacob was born, which truly rocked my world. I didn't share this with anyone until months later. I thought it was just another ball to juggle and didn't want to bother anyone. I remember one night months after the miscarriage when I realized I was just so angry – with God, with the loss, with my inability to "handle" the situation as I had handled everything else in my life. I cried out to God, seeking the comfort and strength to process the loss, but I was still trying to be "perfect." I was pushing my body to the limit. I ended up in the hospital with a serious lung abscess. God healed me, but I realized I needed something to change.

The Pace of Grace

Sometime during this season our beautiful daughter Natalie was born and I was overjoyed. But the juggling was getting harder, and my Energizer Bunny persona was failing me. I remember the moment I realized that I could not keep going and going and going, nor could I keep all the balls in the air for too much longer. I knew that I did not have the solution, but was certain that I had to come up with one. So I cried out to God and He answered in an unusual way. He brought a book into my life that would change the way I lived and processed things. Steven Covey and his book *The 7 Habits of Highly Effective People* became my best friend. Learning to be proactive, to begin with the end in mind, and live out of quadrant 2 and my circle of influence recharged my battery. God used the principles in this book to reframe my thinking and refocus my energy. I recommend you buy this book and incorporate these habits into your life.

My husband has always been able to see the big picture. He had tried to coach me to slow down and to do one thing at a time. He uses phrases like "give some energy to it" and "work at a pace you can keep up all day." My former self chafed at these thoughts. I thought the only speed to accomplish something was the highest and fastest. Covey tells a story of a person working hard to clear a forest only to find it was the wrong one. I slowed down and began to "give some energy" to the mission and call God had on my life at a new pace. I called this *The Pace of Grace*. This wasn't energy fueled by my perfectionistic, “I can do it myself” mindset. It was energy fueled by the Holy Spirit. It came with a clear mission and focused vision. I was learning to say yes to the things God asked me to do and no to those that needlessly drained the energy I needed to do the “important things” the "in season" things. And for those extra busy seasons that required more energy, I learned to store up that energy by resting ahead of time. I found ways to work smarter.

The following are a few principles I learned during this season.

1. **You need FUEL to stay energized**

Each part of us requires different fuel. To keep your spirit strong, you need to receive Jesus as your Savior and stay connected to God on a daily basis by reading your Bible, praying, and interacting with the Holy Spirit, and you need continual fellowship with the Body of Christ. Occasional visits to church won't cut it. Regular and committed attendance in a local church ensures that your leaders can speak into your life; it's where close friendships are established, and where you can serve God and others.

Thankfulness will also fuel your journey. When you are grateful and content with what you have, it will energize you to keep moving forward. The Bible encourages us to give thanks in all circumstances. William Wordsworth told people to rest and be thankful. That is a winning combination!

To keep your soul strong, you need the fuel of strong, healthy friendships. You need to stay mentally and physically energized by continually learning, growing, and exercising. In his book, Steven Covey uses the concept of keeping your saw sharp. It takes much more energy to saw a log with a dull saw. You need to keep your saw sharp spiritually, emotionally, physically, relationally, and mentally. As I shared earlier, this was a lesson I learned the hard way. This Scripture from Colossians says it well:

"So we have not stopped praying for you since we first heard about you. We ask God to give you complete knowledge of his will and to give you spiritual wisdom and understanding. Then the way you live will always honor and please the Lord, and your lives will produce every kind of good fruit. All the while, you will grow as you learn to know God better and better. We also pray that you will be strengthened with all his glorious power so you will have all the endurance and patience you need. May you be filled with joy,

always thanking the Father. He has enabled you to share in the inheritance that belongs to his people, who live in the light. For he has rescued us from the kingdom of darkness and transferred us into the Kingdom of his dear Son, who purchased our freedom and forgave our sins." Colossians 1:9-14 NLT

2. **You need a MINDSET that is energetic**

Lethargy is the absence of energy. By definition it is a lack of energy and enthusiasm. Some synonyms are sluggishness, inactivity, lifelessness, laziness, idleness, sloth, apathy, passivity, weariness, tiredness, fatigue, and slowness. None of these sound very positive. I can't control everything in my life, but I can choose how I think and the attitude and mindset I am going to live my life with. Colossians has more to say on how we are to live our lives. This is from the Message Bible and it is quite descriptive:

"Let the peace of Christ keep you in tune with each other, in step with each other. None of this going off and doing your own thing. And cultivate thankfulness. Let the Word of Christ—the Message—have the run of the house. Give it plenty of room in your lives. Instruct and direct one another using good common sense. And sing, sing your hearts out to God! Let every detail in your lives—words, actions, whatever—be done in the name of the Master, Jesus, thanking God the Father every step of the way. Servants, do what you're told by your earthly masters. And don't just do the minimum that will get you by. Do your best. Work from the heart for your real Master, for God, confident that you'll get paid in full when you come into your inheritance. Keep in mind always that the ultimate Master you're serving is Christ. The sullen servant who does shoddy work will be held responsible. Being a follower of Jesus doesn't cover up bad work." Colossians 3:15-17, 22-25 MSG

I love reading this in the Message paraphrase. Give God's peace plenty of room in your life and sing; sing your hearts out to

God. Let EVERY detail of your life be done in the name of the Master Jesus. If you will do this, then the energy will be there to accomplish the important things, the God-designed assignments.

It is crazy how often we equate working harder with expending enormous amounts of energy and working ourselves to the point of exhaustion. The right mindset will allow you to work smarter and actually have enough energy left for other things, including fun! You must have time for fun. It's fuel!

3. **INITIATIVE is your friend**

Have you ever noticed that just starting something releases the energy necessary to complete it? The word "initiative" means: an introductory act or step, a leading action. It is the readiness and ability to initiate action or make a decision. Be a person that puts the ball in play. In the words of NIKE, "Just do it."

I enjoy reading biographies and one thing I notice about people who accomplish what they set out to do is that they take initiative. They come from all walks of life and personalities, but they are all people of action. Sometimes the hardest but best thing is just to start even if you start slowly or poorly. You can keep improving, learning, growing, but if you are stalled you won't make any progress.

4. **You need a life map**

Setting out without a clear sense of direction or destination will keep your wheels spinning with very little progress! I have been doing a lot of thinking about this lately. I have the privilege of being in a later season of life. My four kids are adults. Three of the four are happily married and are all serving God with purpose and joy. Our fourth son Johnny is finishing college and serving God joyfully; I am incredibly blessed. But this didn't happen by accident. Steve and I both made a specific decision in our youth to serve God passionately with our whole heart. We were intentional in waiting for God to connect us with a life partner that was going the same direction with the same heart to follow God. We set our course to be parents who took seriously our job to raise our children to be the "Daniel" and "Esther" of their generation. Of course we made mistakes and got off course, but because we had a strong compass set by staying in God's Word and connected to our local church for counsel, we were able to make progress and reach our intended destination.

This isn't rocket science. It is living a principle-centered, purpose-driven life. It is as simple as following a map to reach your destination and not just winging it. Of course there can be difficulties and detours along the way, but the trajectory and percentage for success is so much higher. Ask God for a clear mission and destination. Set goals and write out a life map. Don't be afraid to ask for help, from God and from others who are headed in the same direction. Vision will energize you and keep you from the draining power of aimless living.

5. **Fun is not frivolous**

Laughter really is the best medicine. I remember a season of stress I was walking through. There were many things that contributed to it, but I was wound so tight, it was dangerous! I was teaching an evening Bible college at the time, but only one class so I was able to go home a little earlier than usual. There was a TV series at the time called Baby Bob. It only lasted 2 seasons with rather mediocre ratings, but for me, it was a hit. I would rush home from teaching, throw on my pajamas and climb into my bed. The show would already be started, but I didn't care. I laughed through the whole rest of the episode. Baby Bob was a six-month-old baby who could talk, and I think he saved my life. All the stress melted away as I laughed myself whole.

In Nehemiah, the children of Israel were given some great advice. They had come out of captivity and were working hard to rebuild their temple and the city walls. They were gathering together to read God's Word and some of them were stressed and sorrowful. Here is what they were told in Nehemiah 8:10 "*And Nehemiah continued, "Go and celebrate with a feast of rich foods and sweet drinks, and share gifts of food with people who have nothing prepared. This is a sacred day before our Lord. Don't be dejected and sad, for the joy of the Lord is your strength*!"

The joy of the Lord IS your strength. And according to Proverbs 17:22, "*A merry heart does good like medicine*." Sing, sing your hearts out to God. Fun is not frivolous or nonessential. It is fuel and it can be holy! God rejoices over us and wants us to rejoice. Zephaniah 3:17 *says, "The Lord your God in your midst, The Mighty One, will save; He will rejoice over you with gladness, He will quiet you with His love, He will rejoice over you with singing."*

This can range from calm happiness to exuberant dancing for joy. We are daughters of the king. He is our joy. and He is our strength. Let's be energized in the right way, with the right fuel. Let's allow the Holy Spirit to live in us and through us and be a beautiful display of God's goodness for all to see and experience.

6. **Rest is your friend**

It may sound counterintuitive, but rest is essential to stay energized. Working smarter includes living with a healthy margin. One of the Ten Commandments is to remember the Sabbath day and keep it holy. There are different thoughts about what this means, but one interpretation is that we are commanded to take regular "Sabbath" rests. This was a hard lesson for me to learn. I had only one speed and it was overdrive. I actually found my sense of worth in how hard and long I worked.

I know a good work ethic is important, but an equally good rest ethic is important too. Burnout is real and comes with a sense of emotional, physical, and even relational exhaustion. You can work yourself into a place where you forget why and what you are working for. I would work myself to the point of physical illness where I would have to take week-long stretches of time to get well. I finally realized that my out-of-balance work habits were actually costing me more than they were paying when it came to time, health and joy. I finally learned that taking the time to sharpen my saw, refuel and restore my physical, emotional, spiritual, and relational self resulted in my working smarter and accomplishing so much more. Even the Energizer Bunny needed time to recharge, even though the marketing professionals wanted us to believe it could keep going forever

God created the heavens and earth in six days, and then He rested! He commanded us to honor the Sabbath, and I believe it is more than a particular day of the week: It is a principle of rest and trust in God to replenish us for the whole journey. There is some good information about how to rest and refresh properly. Steven Covey has helpful information in his *7 habits* book, and Wayne Cordeiro wrote an excellent book detailing his journey in this area. It is called *Leading on Empty*. I encourage you to consider some ideas that will work for you, and then implement them in your life. I finally did, and it made all the difference in the world.

Steve and I regularly took time for rest and refreshing times while our kids were growing up. Now we work hard to schedule precious time with our kids and grandkids, and we guard these moments. Family time fuels us, so when we miss out on that time, we can tell the difference, and quickly readjust. One practical way we implemented this as a principle was by taking good vacations. When our kids were young that usually meant camping or day trips to the coast, but we made this a priority and set time and resources aside to make it happen. I enjoyed planning out our vacations months in advance because just thinking about the time away refreshed me! Nowadays, the planning is more difficult with all the different schedules of our kids, but we manage to make it happen because it is still one of our priorities, and it gives us the energy we need to keep going. We also designed our house to have a restful atmosphere and invested in a matching set of comfy recliners for our bedroom. I keep a small red basket filled with fun things to do – good books, coloring books and pens, embroidery – next to my chair as well. I make sure I plan ahead to rest!

Your rest and refreshing will look different from mine, but it is important that you identify what it is that recharges your batteries. As women, we create the atmosphere of our homes, so let's make sure we are energized and full of joy.

CHAPTER 9:

READY

I love to cook and I have an active imagination. So it's no surprise that I enjoy watching cooking shows. A few years ago, one of my favorites was Rachel Ray's *30 Minute Meals*. I loved seeing her rush around gathering ingredients, then putting out something that looked delicious. So I would imagine that I was doing a cooking show and run around my kitchen trying to put something together in 20 or 30 minutes. I would chop and mix, looking into an imaginary camera telling my own food stories! I know this is kind of crazy for a grown woman to admit, but it did add to the fun of preparing meals for my family!

As I have mentioned, I come from an Italian heritage. Feeding people is our language of love! Most Italian families have their own "long sauce" recipe and are very proud of it. My dad developed lots of good recipes but two that stand out were our "short sauce" and "long sauce" recipes. Both were delicious, but one could be prepared and finished while the pasta was cooking, Rachel Ray style. The other required a full day in the kitchen. Forming meatballs, browning spareribs and Italian sausage, squeezing tomatoes, and putting in all the delicious herbs and spices resulted in what we proudly called "Liquid Gold." Putting all the ingredients together was fun, but tasting and testing throughout the day was the best. There's nothing quite like pulling out a meatball in the not-quite-done sauce, squishing it together and eating it. We made it by the gallons. Hours later, our forks would twirl the pasta as we enjoyed the fruit of our labors. It was ready to eat, and all the time and preparation was so worth it!

Ready! Some things are ready quickly, but most things take time, preparation, and a process. Preparation is an essential practice for God's girls. The destiny that God has for each daughter is different, but the need to get ready for that destiny is the same. So many people think of their lives like a box of ready-made food and want a quick fix kind of life. They don't even want to expend the effort in preparation for "short sauce." But the real joys in life are not without cost. They require time and preparation.

Esther is a beautiful example of this. I encourage you to read her story in the book of the Bible with her name. I referenced her in an earlier chapter because she is such a great example of a beautiful daughter of God. Esther was taken from her people as one of the girls chosen for King Ahasuerus' harem. All the girls were given beauty preparations to get them ready to meet the king. Only one of them would be chosen as the new queen.

When Esther was brought to the place she impressed Hegai, who was in charge of all of the girls. He treated her kindly and gave her special favor. Hegai gave Esther a special menu and provided her with special beauty treatments. He assigned maids to assist her. All of the girls went through 12 months of beauty treatments: six months with oil of myrrh followed by six months with special perfumes and ointments. When it was time for Esther to get ready to go before the king, she was given her choice of whatever clothing and jewelry she wanted to take from the harem. She wisely listened to the advice of Hegai, requesting only what he suggested. Because she was ready, the king loved her more than any of the other women, and she became his queen.

Esther was made ready to take her position as queen. At the time, she didn't understand the monumental assignment God had for her, which was to save her people. But she was a girl who had learned to listen, to take advice from her leaders, and to submit to the preparations that would make her ready. At the end of the age, when the church is presented to God, the Bible uses the example of a bride who has made herself ready. I remember the months of preparation it took to plan for the one-day celebration of my wedding. Actually, it had been years of preparation, getting ready for the one man God had for me. The wedding itself was the celebration of two people being joined together who had allowed God to work in their lives so they would be ready for the adventure of a lifetime. This pattern is seen throughout the lives of those who want to accomplish what God created them to do. They want to be ready because they don't want to fail or miss out on their destiny. The Bible is full of examples of this principle in the lives of countless people who submitted to the process and training required to be ready to fulfill their call. I would encourage you to read Hebrews 11 for a condensed outline of some of these great people. One picture frequently used to describe this process of being ready is running a race.

Picture yourself at the start of a race. This is not a sprint. This is a marathon, a long distance race that will take everything you have to finish. You are not alone. Other prepared runners are beside you. Some have already run the course and are cheering you on. Others are praying for you, and still others are watching to see if you will continue to run, to see if all your hard work and discipline has been worth it.

I am not a runner. The last race I ran was in high school PE, and let's just say no one tried to get me to join the track team! So when I began to write this chapter, I did what all good researchers do: I *Googled* the best position for a runner getting ready for a race. I found many interesting things that runners do to get ready to run their race. They warm up before they run, choose the best starting position, and breathe in extra air before they go. Some additional tips helped me understand more about runners. They don't sprint at the beginning, but instead, they pace themselves for endurance. They watch out for distractions and stay loose, swinging their arms as they run. My favorite statement about runners was that they are to stay humble. The reason is clear: If you are too proud of yourself, then you will think the race is too easy and you will come in at a fairly low position. But if you keep your focus with humility, and just the right amount of self-confidence, you will finish strong.

This is good practice for natural runners, but it also works as we run the race that God puts before each of us. We to need to warm up with daily disciplines like reading our Bible, prayer and worship. Watching out for distractions and staying focused on the race is essential as is staying flexible. Don't become stiff through bitterness and unforgiveness. Staying thankful is like breathing in the positive air of God's goodness. This helps for our daily sprint as well as the lifelong marathons we are running. And don't forget to stay humble! Remember, haughtiness and pride go before a fall, and that isn't good for any racer!

You may think I am taking this race analogy too far, but God used this illustration a number of times to describe our life of faith.

"*Do you see what this means—all these pioneers who blazed the way, all these veterans cheering us on? It means we'd better get on with it. Strip down, start running—and never quit! No extra spiritual fat, no parasitic sins. Keep your eyes on Jesus, who both began and finished this race we're in. Study how he did it. Because he never lost sight of where he was headed—that exhilarating finish in and with God—he could put up with anything along the way: Cross, shame, whatever. And now he's there, in the place of honor, right alongside God. When you find yourselves flagging in your faith, go over that story again, item by item, that long litany of hostility he plowed through. That will shoot adrenaline into your souls*!" Hebrews 12:1-3 MSG

At the end of his life, Paul gave these words of encouragement to his son Timothy:

"*You take over. I'm about to die, my life an offering on God's altar. This is the only race worth running. I've run hard right to the finish, believed all the way. All that's left now is the shouting—God's applause! Depend on it, he's an honest judge. He'll do right not only by me, but by everyone eager for his coming.*" 2 Timothy 4:6-8 MSG

I love this phrase from the Message paraphrase: This is the only race worth running –even with all the suffering. As God's daughters we have a choice to make. Do we take all the blessing and benefits that God has provided for us and settle into our comfort zones? Do we step back into old patterns of thinking and forget our heritage and destiny?

I have used a lot of fairy tale princess movie examples in this book, but this is a book for girls! *Princess Diaries* is another one of my favorite feel good movies. In it, shy teenager Mia Thermopolis (Anne Hathaway) is caught off guard when, from out of the blue, she learns the astonishing news that she's a real-life princess! As the heir apparent to the crown of the small European principality of Genovia, Mia begins the journey toward the throne when her strict and formidable grandmother, Queen Clarisse Renaldi (Julie Andrews), shows up to give her "princess lessons." The movie culminates with Mia scheduled to appear at a formal ball where she will be unveiled as the new princess. As you can probably imagine, Mia gets cold feet as she is overwhelmed by the new call of duty. Her insecurities and fears, as well as the pull of the comfort of her present life, almost keep her from accepting her destined role. Thankfully, Mia presses through the fears and takes her place as heir to the throne of Genovia.

I think most of us can appreciate the struggle Mia faced. We receive Christ as our Savior and embark on our new journey only to discover that not only are we saved, but we are actually daughters of the King. We receive our "princess lessons," learning all that our Father the King has provided for us. But we get cold feet as we begin to understand the responsibility that this comes with, and we still recognize the "common roots" of our humanity. We have a choice. Will we draw back and miss the opportunity to live the life we were created for? Or, will we get into position and begin running the race that will bring us to the throne?

I want to be ready to run, ready to take my place in the kingdom. Let's return to Esther's story. She enjoys her new life as the queen, but soon comes to understand the precarious nature of her reign. She is not to go into the king's presence unless she is summoned. Through a series of events, her people (the Jews) are scheduled to be destroyed. Her uncle Mordecai asks her to go before the king and plead for the lives of her people. She is reluctant and fearful as she has not been summoned to see the king for a while, and does not know how she will be received. She could be put to death if the king finds her actions presumptuous. Her uncle sends her this message: "Who knows if you have come to the kingdom for such a time as this."

Esther agrees to go to the king and the rest is history. The king receives her, and ultimately her people are delivered. But can you imagine how different the story would have been if Esther had not made herself ready? Her success was not an overnight one, but had been built on years of preparation before she was chosen for the harem, and a solid year of preparation for being presented to the king. Esther was not only ready in the physical sense, but also in the mental and spiritual realm. As a result, she made the right choices and listened to the right people.

There are many of our people that need to be saved and need to receive Jesus Christ as their Lord and Savior. We must decide if we have been brought to the kingdom for such a time as this. We need to be ready.

Are you ready to take your throne? Are you ready for the great adventure that awaits you? It will take preparation, and it will take bravery. It will take believing that God is for you, and it will require perseverance. You cannot give up. The stakes in this race are high because you are not just running for yourself. You are running for an eternal prize; you are running for those that will come after you.

I Corinthians 9:24-27 says it this way: *"Don't you realize that in a race everyone runs, but only one person gets the prize? So run to win! All athletes are disciplined in their training. They do it to win a prize that will fade away, but we do it for an eternal prize. So I run with purpose in every step. I am not just shadowboxing. I discipline my body like an athlete, training it to do what it should. Otherwise, I fear that after preaching to others I myself might be disqualified."*

THESE VERSES STIR AND CHALLENGE ME. MY HEART STARTS RACING AND I BEGIN TO GET INTO A RACING POSITION. I DIDN'T START THIS RACE TO LOSE. I DON'T WANT TO DISAPPOINT MY FATHER WHO PAID THE PRICE AND TRAINED ME SO I COULD ENTER AND ULTIMATELY WIN THIS RACE. THE PRIZE IS ETERNAL AND WORTH EVERY OUNCE OF ENERGY I CAN INVEST. I DON'T WANT TO BE DISQUALIFIED SO I MUST RUN WITH PURPOSE IN EVERY STEP. I MUST BE READY!

CHAPTER 10:

THE FATHER'S SONG

September 5, 2015 –The day Steve and I had dreamed of had finally come. She was the little girl with her "I can do it myself" spunk and her two fingers positioned securely in her mouth. She grew up with three brothers and rarely backed down from a challenge. With her pagegirl haircut and soccer shorts, every day was an adventure. She loved practicing soccer with her brothers' teams and was a fierce competitor. As a goalie, she knew how to guard and stop the opposing team from scoring. She loved hearing her dad coaching her from the sidelines, yelling, "Come out of the net." She still loves to hear her dads' voice – both of them. She lives her life with passion, focus and a clear vision for the goal. Now the goal is seeing young men and women's lives transformed by faith in Jesus Christ. She challenges them to live a passionate, focused life as sons and daughters of God. She is a daddy's girl. She and her father share a special relationship, and they always have. He has never stopped coaching her, and he is her greatest fan!

The weeks before the wedding were emotional for both father and daughter, and they couldn't share a lot of quiet time with each other those last days. They knew if they went too deep, it would be all over and they would cry buckets of tears. I remember driving to the church with Steve on her wedding day. We were both feeling the emotion this day brought. He looked over at me. "If I could have just one more day," he said with tears in his eyes. Words of love that spoke volumes about the journey thus far, from bringing her home as our precious little bundle of joy, to this day, presenting our daughter to her own Prince Charming, fresh from

Silverton, Oregon.

She was one of the most beautiful, radiant brides I have ever seen. She told me later that as she and her dad waited to walk down the aisle, he told her to take mental snapshots of this day, these moments. As the doors opened and she began to walk down the aisle, her face was a sheet of tears; thankful tears, thoughtful tears as she took those pictures and reflected on the goodness of her Father God in bringing her to this moment. What a joyful day of promises fulfilled by fathers – two fathers who loved her more than she could ever imagine.

As excited as Steve was to see the beauty of his daughter Natalie as a bride, it is only a thimble-full compared to the joy God our Father feels when His daughters arrive at the destination He has prepared for them. This is not just when we arrive in heaven. I can only imagine what it will be like to hear His voice saying well-done, good and faithful servants on that day. But He rejoices over us daily as we progress on our journey of faith. He sings over us as we move forward toward the destiny and purpose He called us to. He loads us up with favor and benefits to help us succeed.

Psalm 103:1-6 in the Message Bible says it like this:

O my soul, bless GOD. From head to toe, I'll bless his holy name!
O my soul, bless GOD, don't forget a single blessing!
He forgives your sins—every one.
He heals your diseases—every one.
He redeems you from hell—saves your life!
He crowns you with love and mercy—a paradise crown.
He wraps you in goodness—beauty eternal.
He renews your youth—you're always young in his presence.
GOD makes everything come out right; he puts victims back on their feet.

I know that each daughter who reads this book comes from different places, different experiences in life. As you have read this book, my prayer is that your eyes open wide to see the immensity of God the Father's love and plans for you. Jeremiah 29:11 says, *"I know what I'm doing. I have it all planned out—plans to take care of you, not abandon you, plans to give you the future you hope for."*

No matter what your experiences or emotions tell you, the truth is that you have a good Father, a Father who loves you with a never-ending love. As one of the prophets said, He has drawn you with loving-kindness. He wants a personal relationship with you, as a daughter, and He will do whatever it takes to bring you to a place where you can receive that love. It is not something we are coerced into, but rather something we choose. And isn't that something every girl wants - the love and affirmation of her father?

My son Geno made a comment recently that got me thinking. He said, "Not all women are mothers or sisters or wives, but all women are daughters." Think of it! All women have a mother and a natural biological father whether they know him, have a relationship with him or even like him. And, all women have a Father in heaven who knows them, loves them, and wants to have a relationship with them.

The disciples had the privilege of seeing firsthand what a relationship with God the Father looked like by watching Jesus interact with Him. They asked Him to teach them how to pray, how to connect with God like He did. They must have seen something in the relationship between Jesus and His Father that compelled them and made them hungry for the same. The prayer pattern He gave them started with these two words: Our Father. It wasn't my Father or unreachable "far above us" Deity but simply, our Father. Jesus was inviting them into a relationship as family.

Paul spoke of this in Galatians 3:4-7: *"But when the right time came, God sent his Son, born of a woman, subject to the law. God sent him to buy freedom for us who were slaves to the law, so that he could adopt us as his very own children. And because we are his children, God has sent the Spirit of his Son into our hearts, prompting us to call out, "Abba, Father." Now you are no longer a slave but God's own child. And since you are his child, God has made you his heir."*

Here are the same verses from the Message paraphrase:
" But when the time arrived that was set by God the Father, God sent his Son, born among us of a woman, born under the conditions of the law so that he might redeem those of us who have been kidnapped by the law. Thus we have been set free to experience our rightful heritage. You can tell for sure that you are now fully adopted as his own children because God sent the Spirit of his Son into our lives crying out, "Papa! Father!" Doesn't that privilege of intimate conversation with God make it plain that you are not a slave, but a child? And if you are a child, you're also an heir, with complete access to the inheritance."

REFRIGERATOR PRIVILEGES

Daddy, Father! We have been invited into the family as daughters and have complete access to the inheritance. Our birth and adoption was paid in full by the blood of Jesus with the adoption papers signed by the Holy Spirit. We are fully adopted as God's own children. He is our Daddy, and we have the privilege of intimate conversation and full access to all His resources. My husband likes to compare it to the full access "refrigerator" privileges that our children have at our house. I come from an Italian heritage and feeding my family is my language of love. I would be crushed if my kids held back from eating anything and everything that is provided in our home. How much more must it crush our Father God when we act like strangers in His house.

In Italian households, Mangiamo, "Let's eat," or Mangia tutti, "Everybody eat" are frequently heard. I can hear God's voice speaking this to His kids. In fact, Jesus used this example in one of His parables about a wedding feast. In Luke 14, the master of the house sent out many invitations and when the banquet was ready, he sent his servant to tell everyone to come. The invited guests had varied excuses about why they could not or would not come. The master was furious and sent his servant to invite strangers to fill the table. "Mangia tutti, everybody eat," he cried to fill the tables. I don't want to bring excuses to God about why I am not coming to the family table and filling up on the rich resources He has provided. When God says "Come and eat," I'm going to go and eat!

Two songs stick out to me as I finalize my thoughts. One is the song "Daughters"[1] by John Mayer and the other, "The Father's Song"[2] by Matt Redman. In very different ways and from different perspectives they share the importance and beauty of a Father's love.

Mayer shares the beauty and complexities he has discovered in a girl he cares for:

"I know a girl!

She puts the color inside of my world

But, she's just like a maze

Where all of the walls all continually change

And I've done all I can

To stand on her steps with my heart in my hand.

Now I'm starting to see

Maybe it's got nothing to do with me

He realizes that the way her father has treated her has shaped her and he says:

Fathers, be good to your daughters; Daughters will love like you do

Girls become lovers who turn into mothers

So mothers be good to your daughters too...

On behalf of every man looking out for every girl you are the god and weight of her world."

Those are quite profound words. They speak into the crucial reality that fathers matter...big time!

The second song is "The Father's Song" by Matt Redman. I remember the first time I heard this song. I wept as I realized how much my Father God loved me and literally heard a song He was singing over me.

"I have heard so many songs, listened to a thousand tongues but there is one that sounds above them all.

The Father's song, the Father's love - You sung it over me and for eternity it's written on my heart."

As I heard the line, "Heaven's perfect mystery, the King of Love has sent for me and now He's singing over me the Father's song," I was overwhelmed and so moved at God's incredible love. I pictured Esther kneeling before the King when he put out his scepter and sent for her to come to him. God loved and received me like that. When I didn't deserve it, when I had not earned it, He sent His son to die for me so that I could be His daughter forever.

Both songs speak to me again of how important a proper relationship with your father is, especially your heavenly one! God is the perfect Father. If you didn't know it before, I hope that through the chapters of this book you see it more clearly. He delights in you, especially when you are comfortable in who He created you to be. He has an unconventional destiny for you and a glorious place of service and honor for you to walk in. He will continue to train and energize you so that you will be ready to take your rightful place ruling and reigning with Him, in this life.

My prayer for you is this: No matter what kind of natural dad you have, you won't let it keep you from getting to know your

Father God. There is healing and restoration if you need it. These are not trite promises but true realities. I pray you will take time to explore the Bible for yourself and find out everything you can to know God better. Maybe you have never read it or maybe you are a regular reader, but in His words are the answers and the affirmation every girl wants.

God is amazing –

the best Father,

the best friend,

the best everything!

But don't take my word for it.

Go hear Your Father's song for yourself.

ENDNOTES

Introduction

Heward-Mills, Dag. Daughter, You can make it. Christlight Books, April 29, 2014

Chapter 1

Elhage, Alyssa. "The surprising way your father impacts who you will marry" (online). Available Verilymag.com. June15, 2015

Chapter 3

Motti, Diane. "Ways of living an authentic life" (Online). PsychCentral.com.

Chapter 4

Ellicott, CJ. Ellicott's Commentary to English Readers. Nabu Press, 2011. From original 1905 printing

Ulrich, Laurel Thatcher. Cotton Mather quotes.Quoteinvestigator.com.

Chapter 5

Tornquist, Evie. He loves me. 1978

Chapter 7

Stanton, Glen. "The Involved Father". Focus on the family.com .2004

Chapter 8

Information on the Energizer bunny from Energizer.com

Chapter 10

Mayer, John. "Daughters" from album Heavier Things.Columbia. 2003.

Redman, Matt. "The Father's Song" from album The Father's Song. Survivor Records.2000.

Made in the USA
Columbia, SC
10 January 2020

86469733R00059